ENGLISH
for the more able

Mary Green

Contents

Introduction

The series *English for the More Able*, books 1–6, has been written for primary school children whose performance is above their chronological age and who need particularly challenging tasks. It is assumed they will have wide reading experience, a good command of language, have acquired problem-solving skills and can work independently. Intervention by the teacher can therefore be minimal.

Book 2 in the series is targeted at children aged 6–7 years. The tasks included in each activity sheet relate to the objectives in the *National Literacy Strategy*, drawing on word, sentence and text levels, and are divided into three terms. However, the activity sheets do not have to be followed in chronological order. You may wish to use them at alternative times throughout the year, according to your needs.

The material and language tasks selected cover a wide range of subjects, genres and writing styles. For example, 'Floating ships' in Term 1 focuses on writing simple instructions and how to note key structural features, while 'Make a nursery rhyme' in Term 3 looks at the language of nursery rhymes and how to write them using rhythm and rhyme.

The teacher page
Each activity sheet is accompanied by a page of supporting notes giving advice and information about how to use the activities. It is organised under the following sub-headings:

● **Learning objectives**
The skills on which each activity sheet is based are outlined here.

● **Activity sheet/Expectations**
This describes the content of the activity sheet, and elaborates on the objectives above. It also gives the teacher an indication of the kinds of skills required by the children and what to expect from them. Examples are often given and, where appropriate, specific answers.

● **Further activities**
Suggestions are offered on how to develop further the skills and tasks detailed in the activity sheets. These may involve extended work (such as creating a booklet over time), research work (such as using ICT) or shorter tasks.

● **Resources**
This lists the relevant activity sheet, together with information on useful equipment and books, such as poems, reference and other non-fiction texts.

Objectives grid
This appears on page 64, and it provides a quick, easy-to-consult guide to the skills covered in the activity sheets.

Spelling patterns

Learning objectives

Word level
- *The common spelling patterns for the vowel phonemes* and digraphs:
  - *oo (short as in good):* 'u' (as in pull);
  - *ar:* 'ar' (car);
  - *oy:* 'oi' (boil), 'oi' (toy);
  - *ow:* 'ow' (cow), 'ou' (sound).

Activity sheet/Expectations

It is assumed that the children will already be familiar with the vowel combinations listed above. They should, therefore, have achieved a good level of reading and spelling.

The letter on the activity sheet has 12 spelling errors, which the children should identify and correct on the sheet. The correct spellings are: (*Mowse*) Mouse, (*Janury*) January, (*Deer*) Dear, (*Braney*) Barney, (*praty*) party, (*huose*) house, (*cloun*) clown, (*cuck*) cook, (*pool*) pull, (*tois*) toys, (*joyn*) join, (*Mraty*) Marty.

The errors involve:
- reversal of the digraph (as in *praty*/party);
- confusion of the digraph (as in *Mowse*/Mouse, *cloun*/clown);
- omission (as in *Janury*/January);
- incorrect homophone (as in *pool*/pull).

There are several clues on the activity sheet that the children should be able to call on. For example:
- the correct spellings of *party, Marty, Barney* and *Mouse* are included, as well as the incorrect ones;
- the context should help the children to recognise what a misspelled word is meant to be, for instance that the word *pull* rather than *pool* is the correct choice.
(If the children need help with setting out Barney's reply, please see below.)

Further activities

January is the most difficult spelling and the one most likely to be overlooked. You may wish not only to point to the *ar* digraph, but also to show the children that splitting the word into syllables will help them to remember it.

Use Marty's letter to introduce or reinforce the way in which a friendly letter is set out, with the address and date in the right-hand corner, the greeting in the left and the customary signing off.

You may also wish to point to the use of exclamation and question marks and ask the children to describe their functions.

Resources

AS 'Poor Barney!'

Poor Barney!

1. Poor Barney is in a muddle. Marty Mouse has sent him a letter but Barney cannot read it – there are too many spelling mistakes! Correct Marty's letter by writing the correct words underneath, like the example.

~~Mowse~~ Hole
Mouse

3 Janury

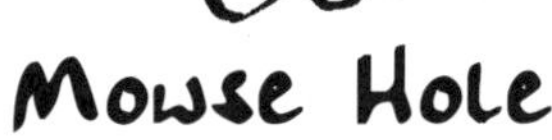

3 Janury

Deer Braney

I would like you to come to a praty at my huose on Sunday. It will be a fancy dress party.

Can you wear your cloun suit? I will cuck some tasty food. There will be cakes to eat and crackers to pool. You can play with the tois and joyn in all the games, too.

From Mraty

2. Do you think Barney will go to the party? Write a reply to Marty.

Homophones

Learning objectives

Word level
● *To investigate and classify words with the same sounds but different spellings.*

Activity sheet/Expectations

In this activity, the children are asked to identify a series of homophones by using pictures as prompts. Since there are no word or sentence clues, the children's spelling should be of a good standard. In particular, they will need to have command of the common vowel combinations, such as *ea*, *oo*, *ee* and *ai*, and the more complex *air*, *are* and *our* (as in *four*). They will also need to be aware of the silent *l* in *would*, *could* and *should*.

Answers: The homophones covered on the activity sheet are: question 1. *pear/pair*, *fair/fare*, *wood/would*, *sea/see*, *bee/be*, *stair/stare*, *sun/son*, *four/for*, *tail/tale*, *deer/dear*; question 2. *road/rode/rowed*.

Further activities

Ask the children to record any words they are unsure of and to write sentences to show the meanings.

Other common homophones you may wish to cover are: *week/weak*, *one/won*, *hear/here*, *no/know*, *fur/fir*, *write/right*, *saw/sore*, *heel/heal*, *steel/steal*, *groan/grown*, *shore/sure*, *to/two/too*, *their/there* (and, if appropriate, *they're*).

Discuss other similar word types with the children, such as homographs (when two words or more look the same, sound the same but have a different meaning and are grammatically different). For example: *bank* (noun) as in the *bank* of a river but *bank* (verb) as in to bank money; *wave* (noun) as in a wave made by the sea/*wave* (verb) as in to wave a hand; *bow* (noun) as in bow tie but *bow* (verb) as in to bend forwards.

Resources

AS 'Follow the road'; pencils

Follow the road

Name: .... **Date:** ....

1. Follow the winding road with your pencil. When you come to a picture, write down its name beside the number 1. Then, beside the number 2, write down another word that sounds the same but is spelled differently. The first has been done for you.

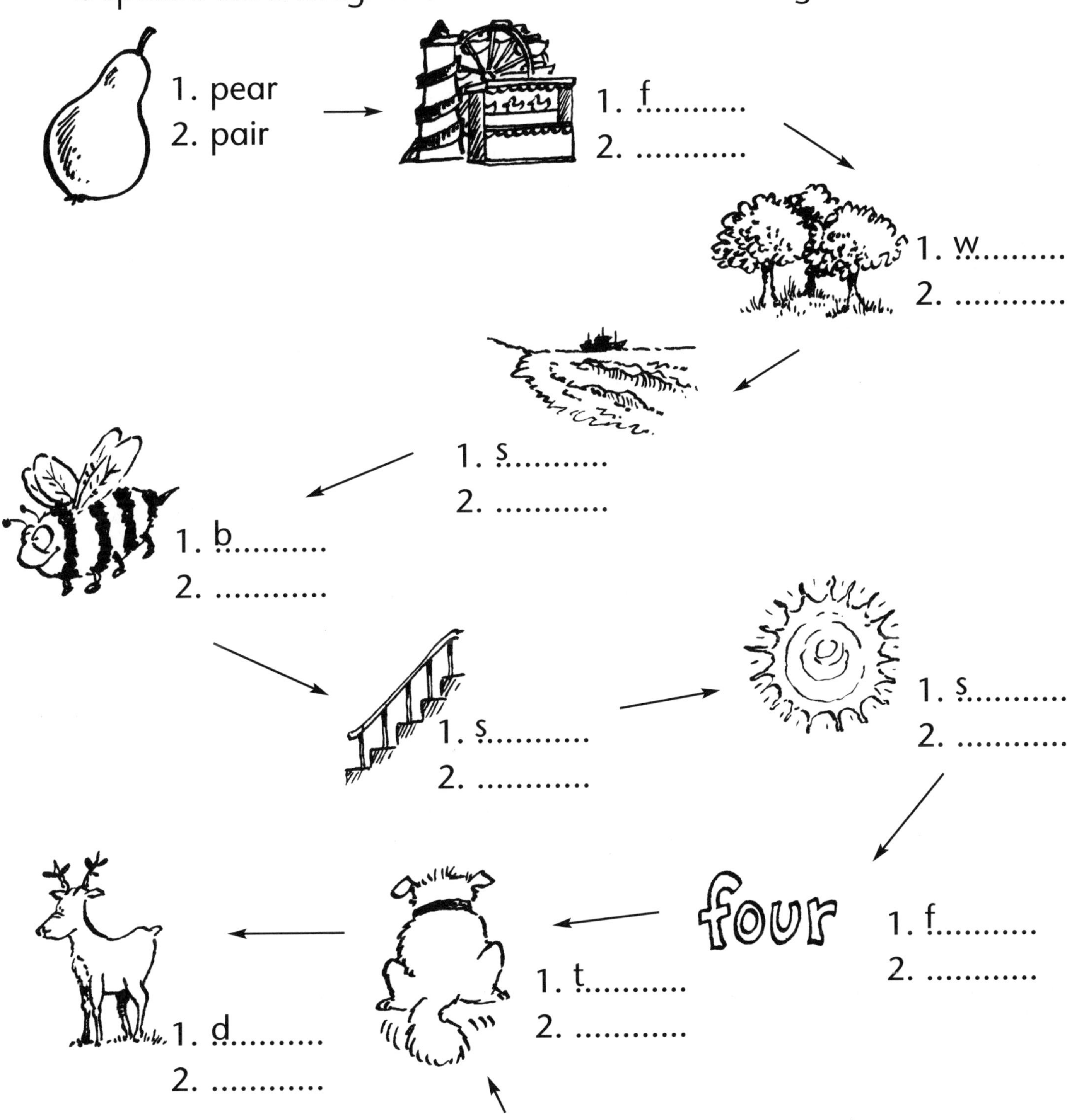

2. Can you think of two more words that sound like *road* but are spelled differently? Write them down.

Capitalisation and exclamation marks

Learning objectives

Sentence level
- *To revise knowledge about other uses of capitalisation, e.g. for names, titles, emphasis, and begin to use in own writing.*
- *To recognise and take account of exclamation marks in reading and own writing.*
- To use capital letters and full stops in sentences.

Activity sheet/Expectations

There are several ways in which the children need to use capitalisation in the tasks on the activity sheet. They should, therefore, have had some experience (if limited) of using them in their own writing, as well as being able to recognise them in reading. They will have to pick up certain cues, such as noting how capitals are used on the activity sheet, and follow instructions (realising that the notices will be signed by different members of the Bud family).

More precisely, the children need to use capital letters:
– to emphasise the commands on the notices (together with an exclamation mark);
– when signing the various names (that is, *Mr Bud*, *Mrs Bud*, *Little Bud*);
– when writing sentences (as well as using full stops);
– when writing the title in answer to question 3.

Regarding the last point, it is useful to note how many children make the connection between the Buds and *The Tale of Peter Rabbit* by Beatrix Potter. If they have sufficiently good reading experience, it is likely that they will have come across Beatrix Potter's books.

The children also have to think of five different ways to say 'Keep out!' Some possible suggestions are: *Stay away! Don't come in! Keep away! Can't come in! Go away! No entry*! *Stay out! No trespassers!* (The last example is quite tricky, but the children may have encountered the phrase on walks or trips and so have some familiarity with it.)

Further activities

Since capitalisation is used in a range of ways on the activity sheet, you might like to keep the sheet to reinforce particular learning points (once the children have completed the tasks), especially those punctuation skills of which they are uncertain.

Resources

AS 'Keep out!'; the original *Peter Rabbit* books by Beatrix Potter (Frederick Warne & Co)

Keep out!

Mr and Mrs Bud and Little Bud are cross! Last week somebody came into the garden and stole Mr Bud's turnips. Yesterday someone dug up Mrs Bud's potatoes. Today Little Bud's carrots have gone! They are each going to make two notices to keep people out.
The first has been made.

1. Write the other five notices in the spaces provided. Think of five different ways to say: 'KEEP OUT!' Use capital letters and exclamation marks. Sign each notice.

2. Who do you think has been stealing the vegetables? Write a sentence to say why.

3. Which famous story does this remind you of? Write down the title and the author.

Organisational devices

Learning objectives

Sentence level
- *To use a variety of simple organisational devices, e.g. ... lines ... keys.*

Text level
- *To write simple instructions, e.g. getting to school.*

Activity sheet/Expectations

This activity sheet focuses on a pictorial map, depicting two routes to the same school, and involves several skills. The children need to:
– sequence by following and giving directions;
– use simple organisational devices;
– write using connectives as prompts;
– relate picture symbols to words by completing a key;
– have good pencil control and write within a limited space.

In addition, the children are encouraged to use a range of senses to reinforce both meaning and sequence. It is important, therefore, that they attempt the tasks on the activity sheet in order so that in the first task touch and speech are emphasised.

The children should be using script and be able to make diagonal and horizontal joins in order to complete the sentences in the spaces provided. They should also try to include references to left and right when completing the sentences. For example:

> Sam walks down Dove Park Road.
> Then he turns left into Sparrow Lane.
> At the bottom of Sparrow Lane he turns right into Blackbird Road.
> At the end of Blackbird Road he turns left into Starling Street.
> The school is at the end of Starling Street.

Note: You may wish to provide a lined sheet of paper for the children to place under the activity sheet to help them to write clearly.

Further activities

Mila and Sam's routes meet at Blackbird Road. Ask the children to identify this point on the map and to mark it with a cross. Then note whether or not the children can spot that all the roads on Sam's route are named after birds. The children can also add other picture symbols (such as houses) onto the map and record them in the key. Finally, ask them to draw a compass for the map. (Pictorial maps of varying complexity can be made available for the children to study. These can often be obtained from tourist information offices.)

Resources

AS 'Getting to school'; pencils; pictorial maps (if possible); lined sheets of paper (optional)

Getting to school

Name: .... **Date:** ....

1. Mila and Sam are friends. They live in the same town but in
different areas. Follow the route that Mila takes to school. Say the
names of the places as you go.

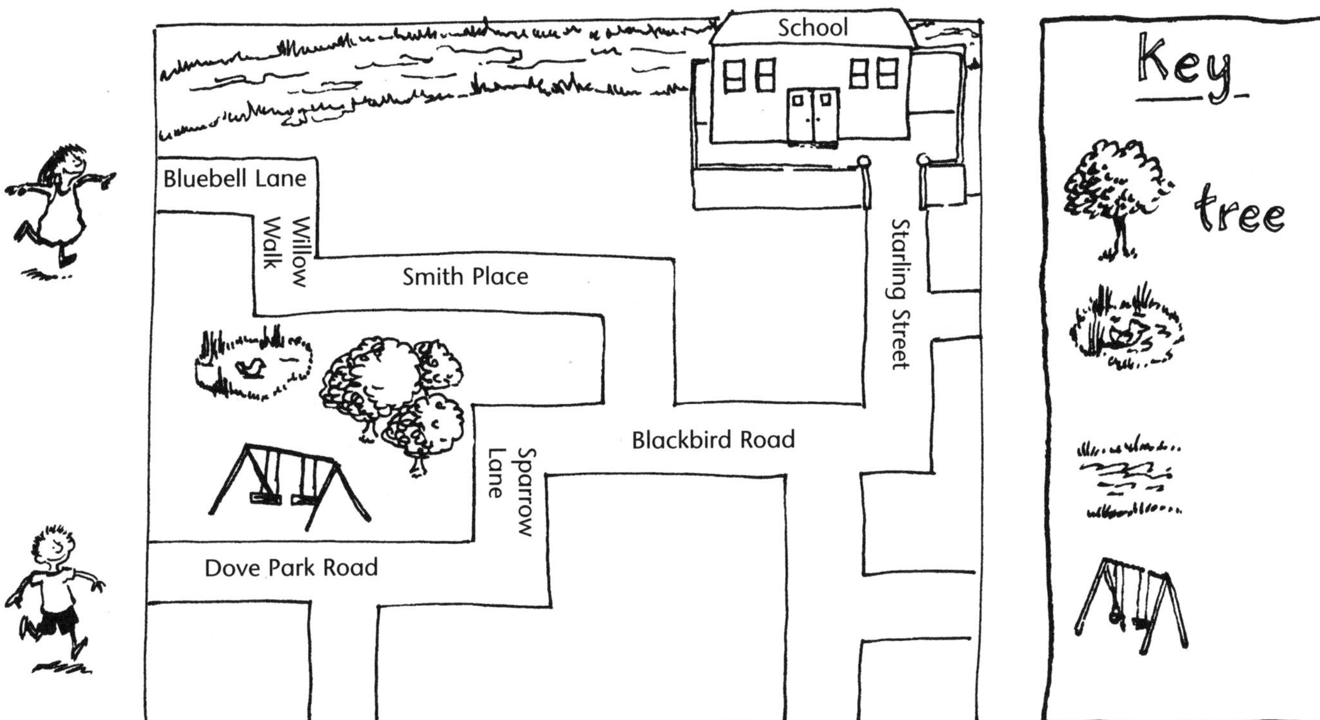

2. Use a pencil to trace the route you think Sam takes to school.

3. Finish these sentences to describe how he does it.

Sam walks down..Road.

Then he turns ....

At the bottom ....

At the end ....

The school ....

4. Now write down the words to finish the key.

Following a story

Learning objectives

Text level
- To understand time and sequential relationships in stories, i.e. what happened when.

Sentence level
- *To find examples, in fiction ... of words and phrases that link sentences, e.g. after, meanwhile, during.*
- To understand that most stories have a message or a moral.

Activity sheet/Expectations

The passage on the activity sheet, 'The fox and the lion', has been adapted from the fable by Aesop and contains a simple message: 'Familiarity can overcome fear.' However, the children might understand this more easily as: 'It is better to be friends than enemies.'

The children should be reading confidently at this stage. The story has a readability level of approximately eight years, so children who are reading at a level above this should be able to read it without hesitation. They should read the story without teacher assistance, but you may prefer them to read and discuss its meaning in pairs before completing the tasks on the activity sheet.

The children are asked to identify the moral of the fable and also the story structure (as opening cues in each paragraph) in order to write a similar tale of their own. They may wish to develop this in several ways, but they should try to include some kind of message. The children can discuss the messages with each other once the stories are complete.

Further activities

The story can be used in several ways. You could, for example, point to connectives that link phrases and sentences within a paragraph. The following examples may be useful:
Paragraph 1: *But, and*;
Paragraph 2: *along, into, Suddenly, in front*;
Paragraph 3: *As, But this time, so*;
Paragraph 4: *when, Instead*;
Paragraph 5: *and so*.

You can also point to the use of particular punctuation in the story, such as commas, exclamation marks and question marks.

The children could then identify common structural patterns, language and sequences in a range of traditional folk and fairy tales that you provide.

Resources

AS 'The fox and the lion'; *Aesop – The Complete Fables* (Penguin Classics) and other traditional folk and fairy tales

The fox and the lion

1. Read this story.

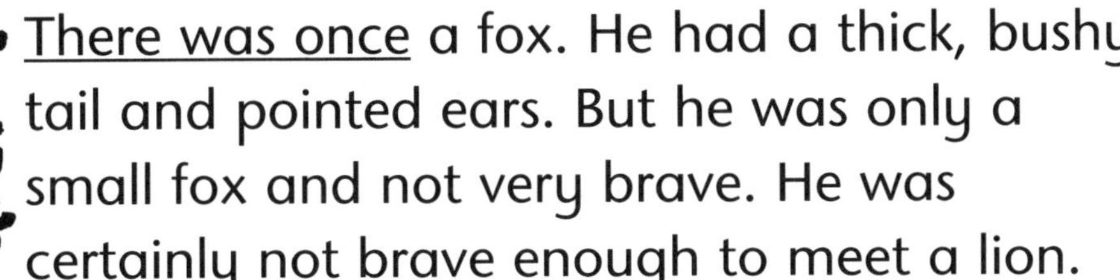

There was once a fox. He had a thick, bushy tail and pointed ears. But he was only a small fox and not very brave. He was certainly not brave enough to meet a lion.

One day Fox was trotting along the path into the forest. Suddenly, he stopped. He blinked. He shook with fear. There, in front of him, were four large cruel paws and two sharp teeth. It was a lion! Fox turned and ran away as fast as he could.

The next day Fox was trotting along the same path. As he turned the bend, what should he see again? The lion! But this time his paws were not so large. His teeth were not so sharp. Fox did not know what to think, so he turned around and went back the way he had come.

On the third day, Fox was trotting along the path when he almost bumped into the lion. This time he did not turn away. Instead, he looked at the lion. He saw a beautiful golden mane. He saw four soft paws. He hardly noticed the teeth.

At last, Fox stepped closer. Lion stepped closer. Fox smiled. Lion smiled. Fox stretched out a paw and so did Lion.
"Shall we be friends?" they said together.

Adapted from a fable by Aesop

2. What do you think the story really means? Write a sentence to say.

3. Underline the opening words in each paragraph (the first has been done for you). Then read them to yourself.

4. Write your own story about a cat and a mouse. Use the same opening words for each new paragraph.

Story structures

Learning objectives

Text level
- *To use story structure to write about own experience in same/similar form.*

Activity sheet/Expectations

The activity sheet presents the children with a series of events, as though they had really happened, through the eyes of a child. A simple timeline is also given and the children can use it as a model to write their own accounts. The emphasis is on sequencing events, and the structure is:
– an opening (winning a flight in a balloon);
– development (travelling to the take-off site);
– simple climax (the flight in the balloon);
– ending (landing and recalling events).

Since the children will be writing about their own experiences, albeit in the form of a story, the accounts are unlikely to be sufficiently dramatic to include a complication. However, this can be developed within the story at a later date. (See 'Further activities' below.)

Further activities

You may wish to discuss the structure of the story with the children using the simple terms detailed above.

The children can also develop their accounts into more sophisticated stories by introducing a complication and resolution. (For example, the balloon runs out of fuel, or the wind carries the balloon in the wrong direction and some action needs to be taken to rectify the situation.)

You may also wish to point to the use of connectives in the plan on the activity sheet to show how they link the passing of time: *First*, *Next*, *After that*, *Then* and *Finally*.

You might then extend the discussion of story structures by looking at some of Aesop's fables (those that are suitable for children), especially tales that deal with accepting or being kind to others (see 'The fox and the lion', page 13). Some of these fables are also very short and can provide a simple structure for the children to develop.

Resources

AS 'Up in the clouds'; *Aesop – The Complete Fables* (Penguin Classics)

Up in the clouds

Name: .... Date: ....

Rav has won a raffle! The prize is a trip in a balloon. He has written an account of his trip at school and he is going to read it to the rest of the class. This is how he planned it.

First I will say that I won
a raffle and how I felt.
I will begin:
Last Saturday a letter arrived
for me. The postman ...

Next I will say how we
travelled in the car to get
to the balloon.

After that I will say what it
was like flying in the balloon
and how I took pictures with
my camera.

Then I will say what it was
like landing.

Finally I will say what my
photos were like and what
a happy memory of my trip
I have.

1. What special thing has happened to you? Perhaps you have won something, had a birthday treat or been on holiday. Write about it as a story. Use Rav's plan to help you.

Structuring events

Learning objectives

Text level
- *To use language of time (see sentence level work) to structure a sequence of events, e.g. ... suddenly ... after that ...*

Sentence level
- *To find examples in fiction of words and phrases that link sentences, e.g. after, meanwhile, during.*

Activity sheet/Expectations

It is useful if the children complete the activity sheet 'The fox and the lion' (page 13) before beginning this work. This will alert them to time sequences in a story and help them to see how sentences are linked to each other.

The activity sheet 'What can the matter be?' presents the children with a character (and his dog) and a series of scenarios. They are asked to choose one of these and to use it as the main event of their own story. To do this the children must sequence other events before and after it.

Initially they are given help with a story opening. However, the last word of the opening paragraph (*with*) should suggest that the dog accompanies Simon to the park. Other features, such as a bike, might also be included according to the children's choices, but one of the most important challenges for the children is to develop the character of the dog by giving it a name and including it in the events.

To help the children further, a series of time connectives are given on the activity sheet to help the children link and sequence the events.

Further activities

Refer to the children's stories as a way of developing their writing further. For example, you could point to descriptions of the following, as appropriate:
- the dog: young, old, scruffy, mischievous, obedient;
- the park: has a playground, a café, an ice cream van;
- the bike: new, old, given as a present, belongs to a brother or a sister;
- the shoe: expensive trainers, recently bought, precious football boots;
- the purse: contains a great deal of money, has a name and address, belongs to someone Simon knows.

The children can also work in pairs to study the connectives used by each other and expand their repertoire.

Resources

AS 'What can the matter be?'

What can the matter be?

Name: .... **Date:** ....

1. What happened to Simon? Choose a box and tick it.

2. Write a story about what happened to Simon. To begin your story,
write down the following words.

*It was Saturday. The sun was bright and beautiful. Simon
was as happy as could be. He was going to the park with...*

3. Use some of the words below to start sentences in your story.

When   While   Meanwhile   All at once   Suddenly
Finally   During   After that   At last   In the end

Poetry structures Term 1

Learning objectives

Text level
- *To use simple poetry structures and to substitute own ideas, write new lines.*
- To use structures to write a poem.
- To maintain rhyme and rhythm.

Activity sheet/Expectations

The first poem on the activity sheet, 'When I was out with Jenny', is a variation on a traditional rhyme (of which there are other variations). These kinds of verses, like nursery rhymes, persist in some form or another because they retain the 'English thump'. The rhyme and meaning may change but the rhythm persists. The children should be able to read the first poem with confidence and expression. This is important if they are to feel the rhyme and the rhythm in their voices.

To complete the second poem, 'One, two, three', the children need to:
- identify the *oo* rhyme and match *shoe* with *do*;
- repeat the rhythm of the first three lines so that the poem scans;
- mimic the pattern of words, such as:
  One two three,
  What did you say?
  I said to my friend, we should go out to play.

(It is useful to note here that stress, even in poetry that has a 'thumping' rhythm, can vary with accents and voices and still scan. In the second poem, the line *I saw a bird and a bumblebee* can begin with the stress on *I* or *saw*.) It is best if the children listen to their voices, tap out the beat and ask themselves: 'Does it sound right?' In this way they can develop a good ear for changing patterns. For example, the children should be able to listen to and feel the marked change between the following lines in the first poem:

And	*all*	*the*	*fish*	*that*	*he*	*could*	*catch*
Te	TUM	te	TUM	te	TUM	te	TUM

Were	*one,*	*two,*	*three.*
Te	TUM	TUM	TUM

Further activities

Ask the children to collect favourite rhymes, perhaps from *The Book of 1000 Poems* (see 'Resources'), and to create their own versions using the same rhythm. In addition, you may wish to introduce the children to another version of the rhyme 'When I was out with Jenny', which uses archaic language: *As I went up the garden, I found a little farthing ...*

Resources

AS 'One, two, three'; *The Book of 1000 Poems* with an introduction by J Murray Macbain (HarperCollins Publishers)

One, two, three

1. Read this poem.

> ## When I was out with Jenny
>
> When I was out with Jenny,
> I found a little penny,
> I gave it to my mother,
> To buy a little brother;
> My brother was a sailor,
> He sailed across the sea,
> And all the fish that he could catch
> Were one, two, three.

2. You could use the phrase *one, two, three* to write a poem.
Finish the last line of this poem by choosing the best word from
the cloud below.

> ## One, two, three
>
> One two three,
> What did you see?
> I saw a bird and a bumblebee.
>
> One two three,
> What did you do?
> I tied the laces of my old brown ...

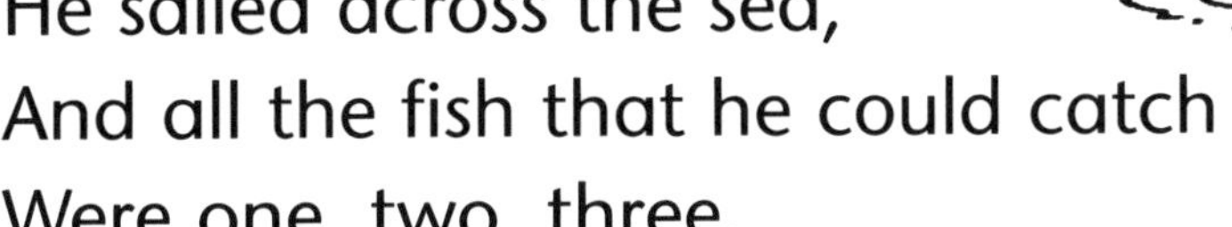

3. Tap out the beat of the poem with your fingers.

4. Add three more verses of your own to finish the poem.

Instructions

Learning objectives

Text level
- *To write simple instructions, e.g. for making a mobile.*
- *To note key structural features, e.g. clear statement of purpose at start, sequential steps, direct language.*

Activity sheet/Expectations

This challenging activity requires the children to use the information on the activity sheet to:
– deduce how the mobile is assembled;
– identify and list all the equipment needed;
– set out instructions sequentially;
– use appropriate instructional language (the imperative);
– use numbered points.

Below is an example of how the instructions might be set out.

> You will need scissors, glue, a hole punch, a drinking straw, paper and a reel of cotton.
> 1. Cut out ship and sail from paper.
> 2. Cut straw to lengths.
> 3. Punch holes in sail.
> 4. Push straw through sail.
> 5. Stick straw to ship.
> 6. Tie cotton to straw and hang up.

Further activities

As far as possible, the children should make the mobile – not only to see if and how their instructions work, but also for their own satisfaction. They can modify the instructions in the light of their experiences.

If successful, the children may like to make a series of ships and design a way of hanging them. For example:
- a straw with three mobiles of different lengths hanging from it;
- a coathanger with five different mobiles of different lengths hanging from it.

The children may like to colour their mobiles and give the ships names.

Resources

AS 'Floating ships'; scissors; glue; a hole punch; a drinking straw; paper; a reel of cotton; colouring pencils

Floating ships

Name: .... **Date:** ....

Can you work out how to make this mobile?

1. First write down the equipment needed
   in the box below.

You will need: ____

____

____

____

2. Look at the pictures and work out the best way to make
   the mobile. Then finish the instructions. Remember to number
   all the points. The first has been done for you.

1. Cut out ship and sail from paper.

2. ____

____

____

____

____

____

____

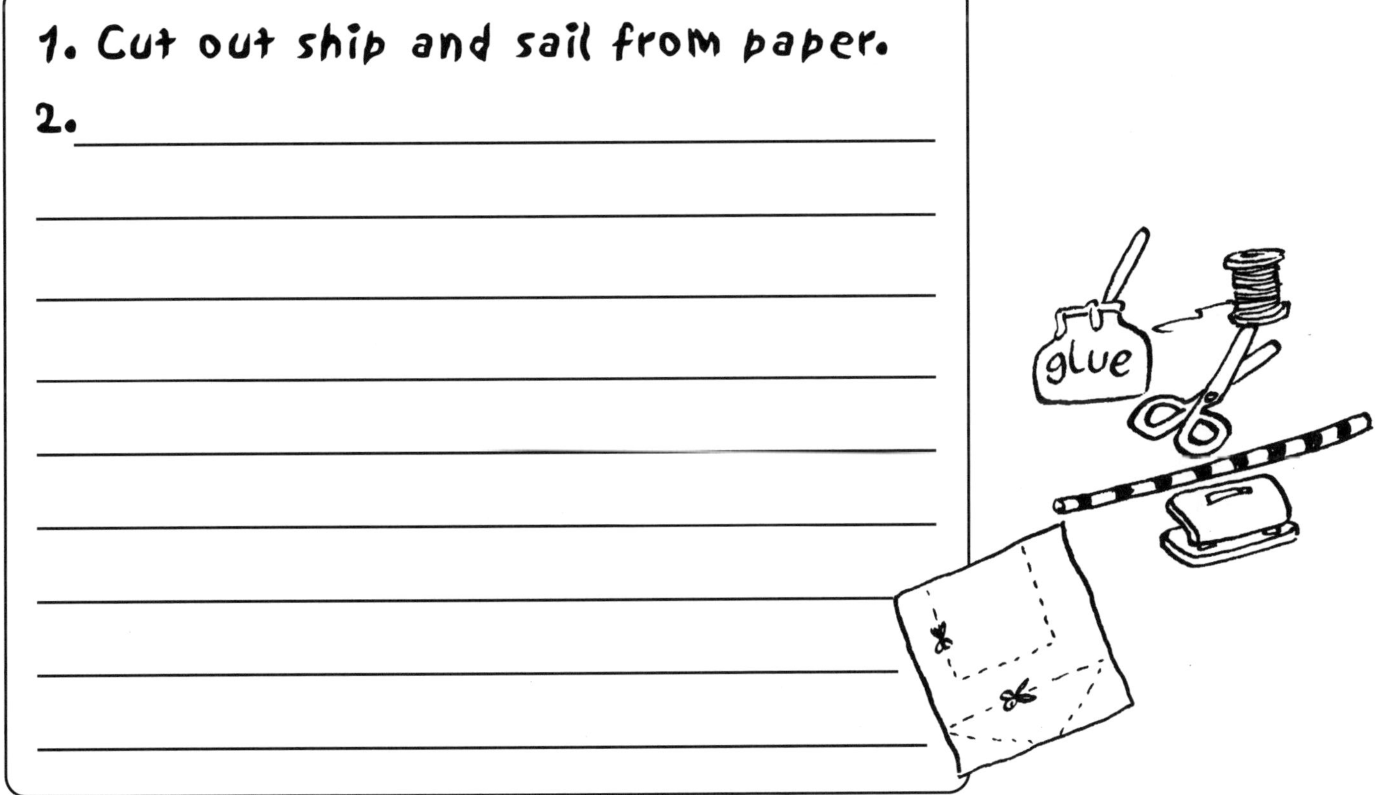

Register

Learning objectives

Text level
- *To use appropriate register in writing instructions, i.e. direct, impersonal, building on texts read.*
- *To read simple instructions in the classroom, simple recipes.*

Sentence level
- *To reread own writing for sense and punctuation.*

Activity sheet/Expectations

The recipe on the activity page, 'Yoghurt dish', may be familiar to many children. (It is often called cucumber raita and may or may not contain tomato and/or onions as additional ingredients.) In any case, the children should be familiar with the language and layout of simple recipes. The children have to:
- write down all the ingredients in the box provided;
- include bullet points;
- use the information on the activity sheet to deduce how to make the recipe;
- recognise that the first sentence of the recipe, *Chop the tomato*, is a cue for using direct, impersonal language (the imperative);
- check their work and tick the appropriate boxes.

The remaining ingredients are half a cucumber, yoghurt and salt, and the remaining recipe might read:
Chop the cucumber. Add them to the yoghurt. Add salt.
Mix together.

Further activities

It is useful if the children can carry out the instructions and make the dish. They can then add to or edit their instructions in the light of their experiences.

You may also wish to point to the instructions on the activity sheets in general and ask the children to decide in what way they differ from those in the recipe. (The language is less impersonal, though still direct, and does not involve the command.)

Ask the children to write out a simple recipe they know from memory, such as making pancakes. They will almost certainly find this challenging and are likely to leave out important elements. However, it demonstrates the need to review and check work, as well as giving practice in sequencing events.

Ask the children to collect recipes from adult cookery books as this can be a useful way to assess how much they understand and how well they use cues.

Resources

AS 'Yoghurt dish'; adult cookery books

Yoghurt dish

Name: .... **Date:** ....

Pip wants to make a yoghurt dish to go with her curry. She knows the ingredients and she knows they have to be mixed together – but she cannot remember what else to do. She has begun the first line:

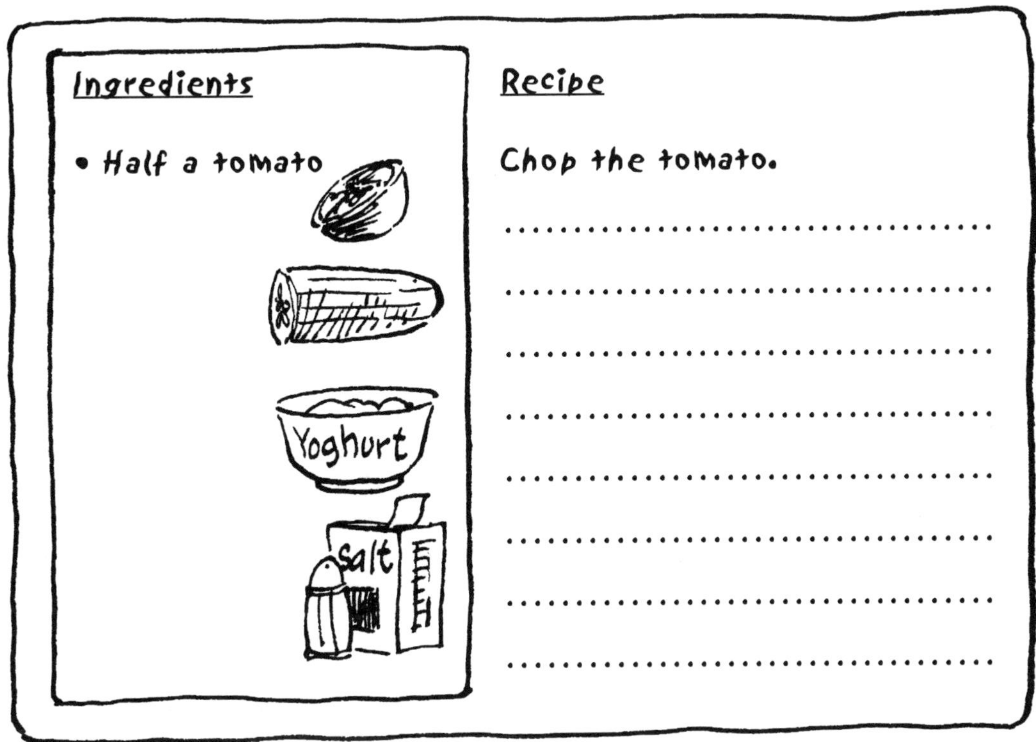

Can you help her to complete her recipe?

1. Write down all the ingredients.

2. Finish the recipe.

3. Give the recipe a title.

4. Read the recipe you have written for Pip.
    Tick the boxes below if you have done what they say:
    ● I have used numbers or bullet points for the ingredients.
    ● My sentences make sense.
    ● I have used capital letters at the beginning of sentences.
    ● I have used capital letters for the title of the recipe.
    ● I have used full stops at the end of the sentences.

Digraphs

Learning objectives

Word level
- *To read and spell words containing the digraph 'wh', 'ph', 'ch' (as in Christopher).*
- To distinguish the sounds from each other and group them.
- To use the words to create questions.

Activity sheet/Expectations

This digraph game, 'Which will it be?', is designed to be played alone, although the children could work in pairs. The object is to classify the appropriate words under their digraphs *wh*, *ph* and *ch* (sounding *k*) and use them to create questions. There are no instructions on the activity sheet, but the procedure is simple and is as follows. The children should:
– close their eyes;
– select a square randomly with the end of their pencil;
– select the *wh*, *ph* and *ch* words;
– record the words in their separate digraph groups on spare paper.

Each child should have six goes and attempt to cover as many squares as possible. (The sheet can be moved around to avoid familiarity with the positions of the squares.)

Once the game is complete, the children can use the words to help construct questions. Sometimes a *wh* word will make this easier. For the squares where there is no *wh* question word, the children must decide how to create a sentence. For example, by using *can*, *how* and *did*.

The words, grouped by their digraphs, are as follows: *where, who, what, when, why, which, whose, wheel, while; Philip, photo, Joseph, phone, elephant, dolphins, phantom, orphan, phase; Michael, Christopher, Christine, school, chemist, ache, chorus, Nicholas, Christmas.*

An example of a question might be: *What time did Philip and Michael get to school?*

Note: The activity sheet can be enlarged to A3 size to make the game easier to play.

Further activities

Note which words the children find difficult. The digraph *ch*, sounding *k*, may prove particularly challenging in less familiar words, such as *chorus*.

Note also if the children have used capital letters and question marks. For example, they should have changed the question words from a lower case *w* to a capital *W*. You may wish to use this as a teaching point.

Discuss other difficult digraphs such as *ch* (sh) as in *machine* and *chef* if the children are reading well and complete the activity page satisfactorily.

Resources

AS 'Which will it be?'; pencils; paper

Which will it be?

Name: .... Date: ....

where false Philip Michael kite windy	photo who frog Christopher spinach winter	children what Joseph Christine famous speech
when phone school kipper Wednesday half	elephant machine wander follow why chemist	kitchen which dolphins office ache Wendy
phantom worry chorus famous whose circus	Nicholas orphan wish wheel circle forest	while phase wink Christmas climb feather

MAE2

Compound words Term 2

Learning objectives

Word level
- *To split familiar and written compound words into their component parts, e.g. himself, handbag, milkman, pancake, teaspoon.*
- To create compound words and make up nonsense definitions.

Activity sheet/Expectations

This activity begins with the children being asked to identify and define some compound words. Once these are completed and it is clear the children understand compound words, they should move on to the next, more challenging, tasks.

The children are now asked to:
- create new compound words from a list and think of their own;
- provide interesting definitions for the words they have created or ask another child to do so.

The game can be carried out in pairs or groups, in which children take it in turns to read out a word and give a definition.

One example of an invented word and its meaning is given on the activity sheet.

Further activities

You can link the work here to how definitions are set out in a children's dictionary, pointing, for example, to additional information such as parts of speech and origins.

You may also wish to introduce the children to the hyphen, showing how it is used to combine words and is often the first stage in the creation of a new word. It is useful if the children begin to understand that language is not fixed and that new words are continually being created.

Look at Edwin Morgan's poem, 'The computer's first Christmas card' (page 61), which plays with language and creates new words.

Resources

AS 'Two-by-two'; paper; a variety of dictionaries, such as the *Illustrated Dictionary* or *Combined Dictionary and Thesaurus* (Folens)

Two-by-two

Name: .... **Date:** ....

1. Read the words below. Underline those that you think are compound words.

> lollipop   rainbow   traveller   pancake   milkman   catnip   lemon

2. Write a sentence to say what you think a compound word is.

____

3. Make up your own compound words and say what they mean! Here is an example.

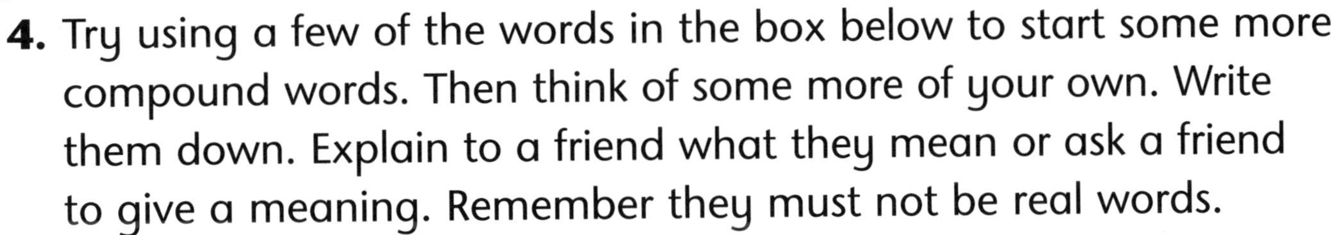

beecage – a metal box for carrying bees

4. Try using a few of the words in the box below to start some more compound words. Then think of some more of your own. Write them down. Explain to a friend what they mean or ask a friend to give a meaning. Remember they must not be real words.

> fan   spin   bag   trumpet   leg   silk   wood   mouse   rag
> cat   camel   red   van   jump   tail   panda   light   shoe

Grammar and punctuation Term 2

Learning objectives

Sentence level
- *To be aware of the need for grammatical agreement in speech and writing, matching verbs to nouns/pronouns correctly.*
- *To use verb tenses with increasing accuracy in speaking and writing.*
- *To identify speech marks in reading, understand their purpose, use the terms correctly.*

Activity sheet/Expectations

There are several skills involving punctuation and grammar here, and the children should have had some experience of using them. As well as fulfilling the objectives listed above, the children should:
- know how to use speech marks for simple purposes;
- recognise question marks and exclamation marks;
- know how to use question marks;
- be able to write sentences in reply to questions and in which verbs and pronouns agree.

On the activity sheet, speech marks are used without written reference to the speaker. (For example, *"Hello Pip! What's wrong?"* rather than *"Hello Pip! What's wrong?" she asked.*) Rather, the speaker is indicated by a picture.

In the first task, the children are asked to reply to a question by using the context and to choose the correct verb part. In the second activity they are asked to supply the question and give an extended answer. In this task they are also given the freedom to write more complex sentences, for example the verb construction might be, *"We have been"* rather than, *"We went"*.

Further activities

You can adapt the work on the activity sheet to demonstrate how this is done, by adding *he said* or *she said* to the speech in the speech bubbles.

Those children who have coped well with using speech marks could be shown how to use them in simple written conversation, as part of a story or short prose piece. This will involve other conventions such as starting a new line when another person speaks.

For those children who need further help, use speech bubbles to present speech and run speech marks alongside.

Resources

AS 'What did you say?'

What did you say?

Name: .... **Date:** ....

Can you remember how to use speech marks?

1. Write down the reply to these questions. Use one of the words underneath in your answer and don't forget to add speech marks.

2. Now ask the triplets a question. Write down the question and each triplet's reply. Remember to use speech marks.

____

____

____

____

____

____

Punctuation

Learning objectives

Sentence level
- To use commas to separate items on a list.
- *To read aloud with intonation and expression.*
- To use commas in sentences.
- To write using exclamation marks appropriately.
- To write using question marks appropriately.

Activity sheet/Expectations

A range of punctuation has been removed from different kinds of writing on the activity sheet and the children are asked to make corrections. The examples cover several contexts: a list, a letter, captions and an email.

The children need to be observant to note carefully what is missing, as well as being able to understand what kind of punctuation is required. Simple clues are given through the picture symbols, and the children are asked to read the examples with expression when the work is completed, which may also provide a check.

Punctuation should be added as follows:
- Ricky's schoolbag list: commas separating items on a list;
- Gran's note: comma after *Dear Ricky*, question mark at the end of the first sentence, commas separating items on a list, comma after *Thanks*;
- Ricky's drawings: exclamation marks;
- Auntie's email: comma after *Dear Ricky*, question mark after second sentence.

Further activities

Point to the use of the exclamation mark in the instructions on the activity sheet and ask the children why they think it has been used.

Ask the children to write replies to Gran's letter and Auntie's email, using appropriate punctuation. Where possible, give the children opportunities to see and use genuine emails. You can point to some of the differences between books and technology by contrasting, for example, turning pages and scrolling on a screen.

The children can also draw up lists and reminder notes for their own use, again using appropriate punctuation.

Resources

AS 'Ricky'; sample emails; computer for internet connection (optional)

Ricky

1. The punctuation has run away from the sentences in these notes!
Put it back in the right places.

Ricky s schoolbag list
pen pencils rubber ruler
reading book sharpener

Gran s note
Dear Ricky
Can you please buy some food for me
I need milk eggs butter cheese and tea.
Thanks
Gran

Ricky s drawings

Auntie s email
Dear Ricky
I arrived safely at 7 o'clock.
Did you get home okay

Auntie

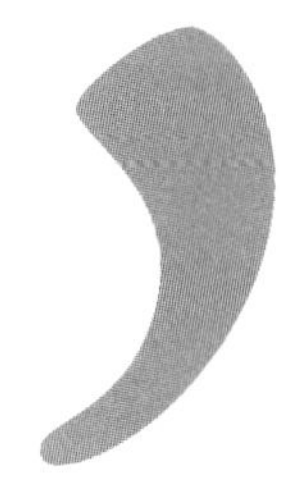

2. Now read all the examples aloud with expression. Have you added
all the punctuation?

Patterns of rhythm and rhyme

Learning objectives

Text level
- *To identify and discuss patterns of rhythm, rhyme and other features of sound in different poems.*
- *To use structures from poems as a basis for writing, by extending or substituting elements, inventing own lines, verses; to make class collections, illustrate with captions; to write own poems from initial jottings and words.*

Activity sheet/Expectations

Valerie Bloom's poem, 'Sly Mangoose', can be read aloud by the children for pleasure and they can discuss the characters of the mother hen and the mongoose.

The children can then work alone or in pairs to locate the rhythm of the poem. They can tap out the beat in the first line, noting where the stress comes, or they can count the eight syllables.

Man/goose	*creep*	*up*	*by*	*the*	*kitch/en*
TUM/te	TUM	te	TUM	te	TUM/te

They are also asked to identify the rhyme (*kitchen/chicken*, *hen/agen* [again] – with the rhyme scheme aabb) and use the theme of the poem to write their own poem. Rhyme is difficult to create convincingly, though the children may wish to try. Some may be able to write poems in the same tongue. Others may wish to write their own free verse poem, and help is given with this on the activity sheet. 

Further activities

The children can use nursery rhyme structures to write their own poems. For example, you can point to the activity page and 'Mousey had a little cheese', which has the same rhythm as 'Mary had a little lamb'.

Ask the children to identify where the poem is set (Jamaica) and, if you wish, point to the different grammar structures.

You might wish to ask the children to contrast the stress pattern in 'Sly Mangoose' with 'When I was out with Jenny' on the activity sheet 'One, two, three'. The children can also find other poems that use similar forms and make a collection.

If possible, look at some of the other poems in *Duppy Jamboree*. This collection contains poems written in the Caribbean tongue and also contains a useful glossary.

Resources

AS 'Sly Mangoose'; *Duppy Jamboree* by Valerie Bloom, from which 'Sly Mangoose' comes (Cambridge); **AS** 'One, two, three' (page 19)

Sly Mangoose

1. Read this poem by Valerie Bloom.

*again

2. Tap out the beat of the poem with your finger.

3. Where does the poem rhyme?

4. Write your own poem about two animals. You can choose to make it rhyme or not.
Here is the beginning of a poem about a cat and a mouse:

Mousey had a little cheese,
Pussycat came by ...

What other pairs of animals can you think of?

Expression and mood

Learning objectives

Text level
- *To comment on and recognise when the reading aloud of a poem makes sense and is effective.*
- To write a brief commentary.
- *To identify and discuss ... features of sound* (alliteration).

Activity sheet/Expectations

Reading and sharing ideas is an important part of the tasks here, so it is best if the children work with suitable partners to complete the activity sheet. Both children should be confident, capable readers who can inject expression into their voices.

They can take it in turns to read the poems and discuss the differences of mood between them. The activities following the poems (in which the children circle appropriate words) should help them to focus on mood.

When discussing 'Bouncing ball' they should consider, in particular, what sounds are suggested, but also what pictures are conjured up and how the poem makes them feel. When discussing 'Is the moon tired?' they should focus on visual images and the feelings created.

The children should try to write short commentaries (of no more than three sentences) on their own, but again it would be useful if they read them to each other and discussed each others' points of view.

Further activities

'Bouncing ball', in part, depends on alliteration for its effect. You may wish to point this out to the children, or ask them to identify the repeated letter *b* and say why they think it is important. They should be able to identify that it emphasises the sound and movement of the ball.

Ask the children to think of words that can create other alliterative patterns. Common letters are *s* and *l* for soft sounds, and *c* and *d* for heavier sounds. They may also note the repetition of the long vowel sounds in the Christina Rossetti poem (*pale*, *vale*, *fades*, *scale*, *tired*, *night* and *white*).

They can discuss with each other how the senses are affected by alliteration – talking about what images, sounds, smells, and so on, are conjured up. You might also like to widen the reading and discussions to other short poems by Christina Rossetti.

The children can try writing their own playground chant, using 'Bouncing ball' as a model.

Resources

AS 'Soft and loud'; Christina Rossetti's poems often appear in anthologies, for example 'Who has seen the wind?' can be found in *Classic Poetry – An Illustrated Collection* selected by Michael Rosen (Walker Books)

Soft and loud

Name: .... **Date:** ....

1. Read these two poems.

Bouncing ball

Bounce, bounce, bounce along,
Blue and bouncing ball,
Bounce along the pavement,
And up and down the wall.

Bounce around the playground,
Bounce about and jump,
Bounce, bounce, bounce,
And bump, bump, bump.

Mary Green

Is the moon tired?

Is the moon tired? She looks so pale
Within her misty vale;
She scales the sky from east to west,
And takes no rest.

Before the coming of the night
The moon shows papery white;
Before the dawning of the day,
She fades away.

Christina Rossetti

2. Circle the words that match 'Bouncing ball'.

soft	loud	thumping	happy	sharp	crisp	sunny
		sad	noisy	cheerful		

3. Circle the words that match 'Is the moon tired?'

quick	sad	ringing	sleepy	jolly	dying	hazy
		gentle	milky	clanging		

4. Write three sentences about each poem and how it sounds. Think about how the poems make you feel and the way you say them. Use some of the words you have circled to help you.

Identifying and using story settings Term 2

Learning objectives

Text level
- *To use story settings from reading, e.g. ... use in own writing.*
- To classify stories by their settings.
- To use a table to classify information.
- To identify story genre.

Activity sheet/Expectations

There are four descriptions on the activity sheet, and each one depicts a different setting and story genre. The children are asked to identify significant features related to the setting of each story and to complete a table. No help or examples are given and the children must work out how to complete what is, in effect, a grid.

The children are asked to add a sentence to each example. This is preparation before choosing the passage they wish to use as a stimulus for their own story.

When they are writing their stories, some children might prefer to combine aspects from the different examples on the activity sheet. For example, A is compatible with D; C might be included in B as an aspect of time travel.

Further activities

Ask the children to identify the story genre of each setting. They should be able to recognise that:
- A is a fairy or folk tale;
- B is a space (or science fiction) story;
- C is a ghost story;
- D is an animal story.

The children could also decide which of the passages are typical of story openings. In particular, they should be able to identify A as a conventional fairy story opening. C and D also signal story openings. You could point out that they provide an introduction to the events that are to follow. B is not typical of a story opening and even suggests that something might have come before. You could ask the children for their opinions.

Look at other related settings, such as those in *How the Whale Became and Other Stories* by Ted Hughes.

Resources

AS 'Story settings'; *How the Whale Became and Other Stories* by Ted Hughes (Faber)

Story settings

Name: .... **Date:** ....

A

There was once a tiny sugar house in the middle of a green wood. It had four windows, a blue door and a red chimney pot, and it was the home of an elf. He was no bigger than your little finger and he was called Pinky.

B

The spacecraft was ready. Gleaming like silver, it stood under the desert sun, ready for take off. Captain Shaw and his crew stepped forward.

C

The castle stood on a lonely hill. It had thick stone walls and four great towers, which almost touched the sky. Every night when the clock struck twelve, strange things began to happen.

D

At the bottom of Mr Smith's garden between the carrot tops and the cabbages there lived a ladybird. Her name was Esmerelda. She liked Mr Smith's garden. The carrot tops fanned her when the sun was hot. The cabbages protected her from the wind.

1. Tick all the boxes that match each story opening.

	hill	wood	desert	castle	spacecraft	garden house
A						
B						
C						
D						

2. Write the next sentence for each story.

3. Choose your favourite and write the whole story.

Character profiles

Learning objectives

Text level
- *To write character profiles, e.g. simple descriptions, posters, passports, using keywords and phrases that describe or are spoken by characters in the text.*
- To identify keywords by annotating the text.

Activity sheet/Expectations

The passage on the activity sheet describes two contrasting characters – a brother and sister – through description, action and speech. The children are asked to isolate the main features by identifying and underlining keywords in different colours. Consequently, organisational skills are also involved.

The readability level of the passage is approximately nine years so the children should be confident readers. There are also some less familiar words included, such as *commotion* and *Astronaut*. In the former the children can use contextual cues; in the latter they will need to depend on grapheme/phoneme relationships, as well as reading experience.

Information on each character can be deduced in a variety of ways. For example, information about Yasmin is given through Mum's comment (*naughty* being the keyword), as well as through description such as similes like *could run like the wind*. The children should be encouraged to underline phrases and clauses as well as single words. They should also try to read between the lines. Yasmin, for example, might be regarded as lively as well as naughty.

When the children complete their character profiles, they should try to construct their own sentences by calling on some of the keywords they have isolated.

Further activities

The children can label their pictures using keywords from the passage that indicate the character's appearance. They can also use the passage as an opening for a story.

If the children are writing well and at length, point to the use of paragraphs in the passage, noting that they signal a change of scene.

You may also wish to point to a range of punctuation used, such as speech marks, exclamation marks and the use of single quotation marks for titles.

Resources

AS 'Chalk and cheese'; coloured pens; paper

Chalk and cheese

Name: .... **Date:** ....

"Come here at once! You are so naughty!" shouted Mum. She was chasing Yasmin around the kitchen, through the hall, up the stairs, down the stairs and back into the kitchen. But she couldn't catch her. Yasmin had sharp, bright eyes, curly hair and she could run like the wind. She was often bad and played tricks on people.

Suddenly the dog, Billy, began to bark. Then Fifi the cat began to miaow, until the whole place was as noisy as a zoo.

Throughout this commotion, Stephen, Yasmin's younger brother, was in the next room. Stephen had dark hair, brown eyes and a small round face, and he was curled up in a chair reading a book. He didn't hear the dog bark. He didn't hear the cat miaow. He didn't hear his mum shout. He didn't hear a thing. He was too engrossed in his favourite book, *How to be an Astronaut*.

1. Underline in black the words that tell you what Yasmin looks like.
2. Underline in red the words that tell you what Yasmin's character is like.
3. Underline in blue the words that tell you what Stephen looks like.
4. Underline in green the words that tell you what Stephen's character is like.
5. Why do you think the sheet is called 'Chalk and cheese'?
6. On paper, draw a picture of Yasmin and a picture of Stephen. Underneath each one write three sentences to say what their characters are like.

Inventing lines

Learning objectives

Text level
- *To use structures from poems as a basis for writing, extending or substituting elements, inventing own lines, verses; to make class collections, illustrate with captions; to write own poems from initial jottings and words.*

Activity sheet/Expectations

The poem 'Song to bring fair weather' comes from the Nootka Indians of North America and is included by Charles Causley in his *Puffin Book of Magic Verse* in the section *Charms and Spells*. It should create an immediate image in the children's minds and is also a useful way to present free verse to them.

The tasks accompanying the poem encourage the children to create their own word pictures by focusing on particular aspects of the weather, starting with the central image in 'Song to bring fair weather'– *a beautiful day of* **rainbow colours**.

The children should try to explore a range of senses and group words not necessarily associated with the weather, such as *bells* and *stormy day*, in question 2 on the activity sheet. The children may wish to work together in pairs or small groups to exchange ideas. Some examples are given below, if they need further help.
A misty day of **pearly skies**.
A rainy day of **dripping trees**.
A snowy day of **silent feet**.
A windy day of **rattling doors**.
A thundery day of **purple frowns**.

Further activities

Ask the children to develop their words and expressions into a poem or poems about weather or the seasons. They can also develop a series of poems together, illustrate them and add them to a class collection.

If you wish to provide another vivid image, you might look at 'Song of two ghosts', again from *The Puffin Book of Magic Verse*.

Resources

AS 'Song to bring fair weather'; *The Puffin Book of Magic Verse* by Charles Causley (Penguin); coloured pens

Song to bring fair weather

Name: .... **Date:** ....

1. Read this poem by the Nootka Indians.

> You, whose day it is, make it beautiful.
> Get out your rainbow colours,
> So it will be beautiful.

2. Think about and note down how the poem makes you feel.
Can you see in your mind a beautiful day of *rainbow colours*?
What do you see in a stormy day of *clashing bells*?

3. Think of the weather below.
Write down some words to finish the lines.

A misty day of ....

A rainy day of ....

A snowy day of ....

A windy day of ....

A thundery day of..

Alphabetical order

Learning objectives

Text level
- *To use dictionaries and glossaries to locate words by using the initial letter.*
- *To use ... alphabetically-ordered texts, e.g. registers.*
- To order words alphabetically to second and third place.

Activity sheet/Expectations

The children are presented with a list of names that they must organise into alphabetical order in the form of a class register. Consequently, not all the letters of the alphabet are included and the children are asked to note this. Names need to be placed in order by locating the initial letter and, in several cases, by locating the second and third letter of the alphabet.

Some help is given with this. Boxes are provided, which are headed with the relevant letters of the alphabet, so the children can make the first selections. However, before they begin the activity sheet and depending on their experience and skill, you may wish to ask them to locate words in a dictionary to second and third place.

The correct alphabetical order of the register is: *Trudy Alan, Jack Angel, Rupert Coles, Frankie Ford, Sally Fox, Maria Gomez, Gwen Jones, Sue Lai, Rebecca Levy, Jenny Macdonald, Jason Molloy, Alex Patel, Mark Peco, William Sands, Kisha Saul, Ruby Smith-Green, Lee Thomas, Dean Watkins, Peter Yip, Polly Young.*

Challenging points which the children to look out for are:
- there is a double-barrelled name (*Smith-Green*) which should be listed by the letter *s*;
- two examples are to three letter places. The first is *Ford/Fox*, the second is *Sands/Saul*. Note also that in the second example there are three names beginning with *s* (*Smith-Green* being the third).

Further activities

You may wish to use the activity sheet to assess the children's skills at ordering words alphabetically. You may also wish to introduce a thesaurus to those who have a good understanding of dictionary skills in general.

Resources

AS 'The register'; *Combined Dictionary and Thesaurus* (Folens)

The register

Name: .... **Date:** ....

1. Class 2 has a register. Can you help the teacher put the children's names in order?

Alex Patel   Rupert Coles   Frankie Ford

Trudy Alan   Sue Lai   Polly Young

Dean Watkins   Peter Yip

Gwen Jones

Rebecca Levy   Lee Thomas

Maria Gomez   Ruby Smith-Green

Jenny Macdonald

Jack Angel   Jason Molloy

Kisha Saul

Mark Peco   Sally Fox   William Sands

Remember:

- the children are listed by their second names;
- not all letters of the alphabet are there.

2. Begin by writing all the names in the correct box. The first has been done for you.

A	*Trudy Alan*	C		F		G	
J		L		M		P	
S		T		W		Y	

Syllables

Learning objectives

Word level
- *To reinforce work on discriminating syllables in reading and spelling from the previous term.*
- To build polysyllabic words.

Activity sheet/Expectations

The children should know what syllables are and be able to break down and build up words using syllables. The task on the activity sheet focuses on building words, rather than breaking them down, and the words that can be formed have two, three or four syllables. One part of each word may be used more than once. (An example of this is given on the sheet.)

This is a challenging activity and the children need to have good visual as well as phonic awareness. The principal words (and those likely to be within the children's experience) that can be formed are: *television, telescope, mission, attention, pollution, mention, altogether, always, permission, person, personal, vision, menu.*

There are others, most of which are unlikely to be familiar to the children, but you may wish to point these out to them when they have finished the task, for example: *viper.*

Note: Tapping out the beat of rhymes and verses helps to isolate and reinforce the syllables. See in particular the activity sheets 'One, two, three' and 'Sly Mangoose'. You may also wish to use this activity sheet in conjunction with the next unit on suffixes.

Further activities

Note any miscues the children have made, for example: *per/mis/son* rather than *per/mis/sion*.

Splitting words into syllables can be a useful spelling aid, particularly if a word is built up mainly of short vowel parts. For example, a word such as *perpendicular* is best remembered in this way. If the children have repeated difficulty with such words, they can record them in their spelling book by splitting them into syllables. It can also be useful for recalling words with double letters, such as *mis/sion.*

If appropriate, introduce the children to the terms: *prefix, suffix* and *root*, pointing out that these are the building blocks of polysyllabic words.

Resources

AS 'Building words'; **AS** 'One, two, three' (page 19); **AS** 'Sly Mangoose' (page 33)

Building words

How many words can you make? Put the parts together. You can use the same parts more than once, like this:

men**tion**   pollu**tion**

tel   tion   **sion**   **per**

at

mis   scope   ten   *poll*

vi   **er**   to   men

al   ways   u   mis

geth   e   **son**

Write your words in the box below.

Suffixes

Learning objectives

Word level
- *To spell words with common suffixes.*
- To spell words with common prefixes.

Activity sheet/Expectations

This is a suffix game in which the children add the correct suffixes to existing words to create new ones. There are six suffixes in all, which help to create words of varying complexity. The children should have some previous knowledge of building and breaking down words using suffixes.

The game is primarily a game for one player and there are four rounds to a game. Using the game in this way means you can focus on reading or spelling. If you choose to use the game for two or more players, the children will need to record the words. The object of the game is to make as many new words as possible. The rules are simple.

For one player:
1. Throw the dice to start. (If a 1 is thrown, the player must begin on the first square.)
2. When a player lands on a square, he/she must make a word using the correct suffixes.
3. Repeat points 1 and 2. The round finishes when the last square is reached – and the exact number must be thrown to finish.

For two or more players:
Play as for one player, but note that a 6 should be thrown to decide who starts and the children will need to write down their words without others seeing.

The suffixes and words created are as follows:
Suffixes: *-ly, -ful, -ness, -ment, -ship, -less.*

Words: *hardly, hardness, hardship, slowly, slowness, careful, careless, kindly, kindness, judgement, useful, useless, agreement, loudly, loudness, restful, restless, harmful, harmless, cleverly, cleverness, peaceful.* Also accept double suffixes from the activity sheet, such as *carefully, harmlessly* and *peacefully.*

Note: You may wish to use this in conjunction with the previous activity sheet, 'Syllables', which involves prefixes and suffixes.

Further activities

Some children may be able to use the game as a model to create a new game in which the existing suffixes and words are replaced by others. This requires breaking down words rather than building them up. The completed game can be given to others to play.

Discuss what parts of speech might be created by adding a suffix, for example, explain that the word *slowly* is an adverb.

Resources

AS 'Word sums'; 1–6 dice; counters

Word sums

Name: .... Date: ....

1 START	2	3	4
hard	slow	care	kind
5	**6**	**7**	**8**
judge	use	agree	loud
9	**10**	**11**	**12**
rest	harm	clever	peace FINISH

Asking questions

Learning objectives

Sentence level
- *To compare a variety of forms of questions from texts, e.g. asking for help, asking the time, asking someone to be quiet.*
- To write questions and answers using question words.

Activity sheet/Expectations

In this activity, the children are going to ask and answer questions based on a picture. The children should write in sentences using the appropriate punctuation and should try to use a range of question words. These questions are not listed on the activity sheet since it is assumed that they will know at least a selection of them. However, an example of a question and reply is given, which the children can use as guidance.

Question words could be: *Who? What? Where? When? Why? Which? Can? How? Shall? Did? Do? Will? Is? Are?*

Examples of the remaining questions and answers might be:
Can I have that toy? No, it's too expensive.
Why are you digging that hole? I'm making a pond.
Shall we go to see the film? Yes, it starts in five minutes.
Will you please keep the noise down? Sorry, but we have to finish this work.
Where is the nearest chemist? It's over there.

The children may misspell words but should not be discouraged from using them. The focus here is on assembling coherent questions and answers.

Further activities

Discuss how the word order alters when the interrogative is used (as in constructions such as *Did you … ? You did.*).

Ask the children to identify a range of questions and answers in picture books. In addition, cartoons and comics are useful for pointing to the use of speech and speech bubbles. They also contain many exclamation marks.

The children are unlikely to use the apostrophe unless they have been shown how to, but they may write a contracted word omitting the apostrophe. You can take this as an opportunity to demonstrate its use, if the children are able to understand it.

Ask the children to provide exclamatory statements for the characters in the illustration. They will need to provide exclamation marks. For example: *Oh No! The train has gone! Ouch! My knee is hurting! Be quiet!*

Resources

AS 'What did you say?'; children's picture books; cartoons and comics

What did you say?

1. Look closely at the picture below.

2. Tick the pairs of people that are talking to each other.

3. In each pair, one person is asking a question and the other is replying, like this:

Q: What time does the train go?
A: It goes in half an hour.

Write down the questions and replies for all the other pairs.
Use different question words.

Authorship and publication Term 3

Learning objectives

Text level
- *To read about authors from information on book covers, e.g. other books written, whether author is alive or dead, publisher; to become aware of authorship and publication.*

Activity sheet/Expectations

It is best if this activity sheet, which is based on the information commonly given in the preface or inside pages of books, is used in conjunction with the next, 'Back cover information', which looks at additional information (blurb) on the back covers of books.

The work is challenging and so the children should be confident readers and writers. In order to write the answers effectively, they should skim through the text first before scanning for particular information. In some instances they are required to make deductions (for example, when assessing correctly how many books the author has written), but in others they need to read between the lines (for example, see point 5 below).

The children should write in punctuated sentences and the following are examples:

Biddy Wells
1. Biddy Wells grew up in Glasgow, Scotland.
2. She lives in a windmill in Devon.
3. She has written a book of poems called *Skyscrapers*.
4. She has written six books altogether.
5. I think she became a writer because she loved making up stories and poems when she was a child.

Other Birdie books
1. Parrot Books publishes stories and poetry.
2. Becky Johns has written two storybooks called *All My Aunts* and *All My Uncles*.
3. Hari Patel has written a story called *Mr Kipper Forgets* and a book of poems called *What the Teacher Said and Other Poems*.

Further activities

Ask the children to look at the additional information given in picture books for small children and try to decide who is being targeted. (For example, note whether they deduce that small children will not yet be reading and that the information is targeted at adults.)

The children can also study non-fiction texts and reference books, and compare the additional information given with fiction, noting if it serves the same purpose. They can also compare the back cover information given.

Resources

AS 'Biddy Wells'; a range of fiction and non-fiction texts, reference books and picture books

Biddy Wells

Biddy Wells grew up in Glasgow, Scotland. She was the oldest in the family. She loved reading and used to make up stories and poems for her five brothers and sisters.

She has also visited the USA many times. It was there she had the idea for the story of her latest book, *Time to Go*. Her other books are *Over the Moon*, *Three Knocks and You re Out*, *Dogs Can Talk*, *Molly and the King s Cook* and a book of poems, *Skyscrapers*.

Biddy Wells lives in an old windmill in Devon. She has a hamster, a rabbit, a chicken, two dogs and three cats. She loves walking and watching videos. She also grows vegetables and has won prizes for her carrots. The carrots are very popular with Bog, her rabbit!

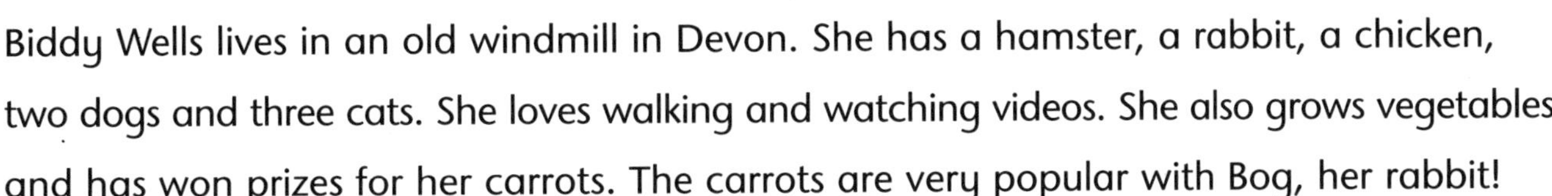

Other Birdie books	**Birdie poetry books**
Jumping Jane by Tom Prince	*Make Me Laugh Again*, poems chosen by Tony Dodds
The Donkey s Song by Bob Scott	*What the Teacher Said and Other Poems* by Hari Patel
All My Aunts by Becky Johns	*Chit-Chat*, poems chosen by Ann Bates
All My Uncles by Becky Johns	*Published by Parrot Books*
Mr Kipper Forgets by Hari Patel	

Now answer the following questions.

Biddy Wells

1. Where did Biddy Wells grow up?

2. Where does she live now?

3. What has she written besides stories?

4. How many books has she written altogether?

5. Why do you think she became a writer?

Other Birdie books

1. What kinds of books are published by Parrot Books?

2. What do you notice about Becky Johns?

3. Who has written more than one kind of book?

Back cover information

Learning objectives

Text level
- *To read about authors from information on book covers, e.g. other books written, whether author is alive or dead, publisher; to become aware of authorship and publication.*
- To write a blurb for the back cover of a story book.

Activity sheet/Expectations

This activity sheet, which looks at the kinds of authorship and publication details usually found on the inside pages or prefaces of hardback and paperback books (rather than in picture books), is best used in conjunction with the previous sheet.

The fictional blurb on the activity sheet mimics the information found on the back of book covers. The children need to understand its purpose – that it not only gives details of the plot and characters to interest the potential reader, but that it acts as an advertisement. (It is therefore different from a review.) The children will need to be confident readers, familiar with texts targeted at older children (approximately nine years plus) and who therefore have acquired some reading experience. They will also need to be able to mimic the style of a blurb noting, for example, that it is written in the present tense.

The children are asked to scan the back cover information for specific facts and to record the details before being asked to write a blurb for their favourite book. Remind them that a good blurb should whet the appetite but not give too much away!

Note: Try to have available a supply of Puffin books and other children's paperbacks. The children can then compare the kind of information given and the way it is presented – factors that vary considerably depending on the audience. (The children can consider, for example, whether it is the children or parents who are being targeted.)

Further activities

Ask the children to write short reviews about books they have read. These can be stuck in the inside cover of the book for other children to read and the activity offers good preparation for writing longer reviews at a later date.

The children can write three or four sentences saying:
– what kind of story it is (for example, fairy, animal);
– what the story is about (noted in one sentence and without giving the plot away);
– what kind of person it would appeal to (for example, an animal lover).

Resources

AS 'Time to go'; a supply of Puffin books and other children's paperbacks; **AS** 'Biddy Wells' (page 51)

Time to go

Name: .... **Date:** ....

1. Read the back cover of this book. It is called the blurb.

Sim and Pop are best friends but Sim is moving to America. He is to live with his rich Aunt Izzie and nobody will tell him why. His grown-up brother has vanished. His parents are in some kind of trouble. Sim doesn't want to go to America. Pop doesn't want him to go. What will the boys do?

Time to go is another compelling tale from one of our best-loved authors, Biddy Wells. Cover illustration by Bill Baker.

Birdie Book Series
Published by Parrot Books

2. Write down the following information about the book.

Title of book: ....

Author: ....

Illustrator: ....

Publisher: ....

Series: ....

3. Write a sentence to say what you think a blurb is.

4. Write a blurb for one of your favourite books.

Playing with nursery rhymes

Learning objectives

Text level
- *To read, respond imaginatively, recommend and collect examples of humorous poems and nursery rhymes.*
- *To use humorous verse as a structure for children to write their own by adaptation, mimicry or substitution; to invent ... own nonsense sentences, etc., derived from reading ... alliterative sentences; select words with care, rereading and listening to their effect.*

Activity sheet/Expectations

Apart from being enjoyable, nursery rhymes are useful models for children to use, particularly when they are attempting to rhyme. Nonsense verse, although it is grammatically logical, accommodates contrary meanings and a range of rhymes that might otherwise not fit.

Alliteration is also emphasised and often adds humour to the verse. 'Mary had a little lamb' probably dates from the early nineteenth century and 'Hey diddle, diddle' dates as far back as the sixteenth century.

'Hey diddle, diddle' has a more complex metre and rhyme scheme than 'Mary had a little lamb', and the children are initially given some help with rhyme. However, they should tap out the beat themselves and try to mimic it. As they become more adept at creating their own nursery rhymes, they should need less help. Below is an example of a rhyme using the words suggested on the activity sheet. You may wish to show it to the children.

Hey diddle, diddle,
I've a pain in my middle,
The camel put on his new hat,
The little fish sang,
In the apple tree,
And the pig danced a jig with the rat.

Those children who have connections with other cultures may like to call on other rhymes and share them with the class.

Further activities

The children can create their own book of alternative nursery rhymes over a period of time, either alone or as a group. The original can be written alongside the new rhyme and the children can illustrate their work or make suitable collages using pictures from magazines.

There are three more verses to 'Mary had a little lamb', which the children could try to find.

Resources

AS 'Make a nursery rhyme'; a collection of nursery rhymes and verses, for example the *Oxford Book of Nursery Rhymes* (OUP)

Make a nursery rhyme

Name: .... Date: ....

1. What nursery rhyme does this come from? Say it to yourself.

Mary had a little lamb,
He had a sooty foot,
And into Mary's bread and jam,
His sooty foot he put.

2. Now say the nursery rhyme 'Hey diddle, diddle'.
Change some of the words. The first line has been started for you

Here are some more words to help you with your rhyme
or think of your own.

3. Find another nursery rhyme and use its style to write your own.

Wordplay

Learning objectives

Text level
- *To discuss meanings of words and phrases that create humour and sound effects in poetry, e.g. wordplay, calligrams.*
- *To use humorous verse as a structure for children to write their own by adaptation, mimicry or substitution; to invent own riddles, language puzzles ... etc. derived from reading; write tonguetwisters or alliterative sentences; select words with care, rereading and listening to their effect.*

Activity sheet/Expectations

The three main activities on the sheet can be done separately; however, it is best if the children work in suitable pairs to discuss the meaning of the verses and how sound effects are created. They can also read the poems to each other, test out their own poems and share ideas.

'Algy met a bear' was voted one of the most popular verses among children. It relies on simple but effective humour and, like nursery rhymes, sticks in the mind. Using the verse as a springboard, the children can discuss their own favourites and why they like them. These might be nursery rhymes, playground chants, rhymes from other cultures or verses from pop songs. The children can try to record these from memory and read them to each other.

The verse in the second activity is like a riddle that uses letters. To understand it requires a leap of imagination on the children's part and an ability to grasp simple puns. They should make the connections between: *A/Hay, Bs/bees, C/sea*. In the third task, the matching words are: *R/are, T/tea, U/you, W/double you, Y/why*, and examples of lines might be: *RU coming to T? W, double me.*

The following well-known rhyme may be familiar to the children and is something of a tongue twister:

2YUR		*Too wise you are,*
2YUB	→	*Too wise you be,*
ICUR		*I see you are*
2Y for me.		*Too wise for me.*

When creating calligrams, the children should be encouraged to use the letters rather than draw pictures. They can add a few lines as needed later.

Further activities

Extend this exploration of wordplay and poetry by introducing the children to other poetry books. For example, you might try *Up to the Stars* – a collection of favourite poems chosen by children and published in association with the Federation of Children's Book Groups.

Resources

AS 'Playing with words'; *Up to the Stars* (Hodder Children's Books in association with the Federation of Children's Book Groups)

Playing with words

Name: .... Date: ....

Read this poem.

Algy met a bear,
A bear met Algy.
The bear was bulgy,
The bulge was Algy.

1. Do you know any short poems or songs? Write one down.

2. Read these lines. Can you work out what they mean?

A for horses,
Bs that buzz,
And C we sail upon ...

3. Which words sound like these letters?

R T U W Y

4. Choose some letters and make up some lines.

5. What has happened to these words?

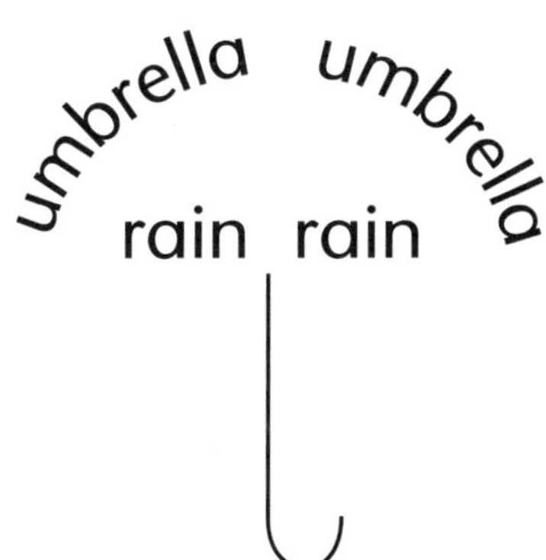

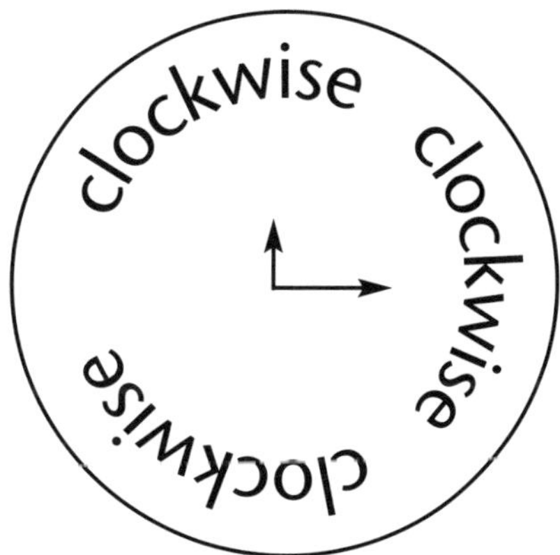

6. Draw the following words so they look like their meaning.

Practise first, then give them to a friend to work out.

falling water   tall tower

Jokes

Learning objectives

Text level
- *To discuss meanings of words and phrases that create humour.*
- *To invent own jokes, nonsense sentences, etc.*
- To understand what 'a play on words' is.
- To understand what 'double meaning' is.

Activity sheet/Expectations

The jokes on the activity sheet should be understood by most able children and can be used as models for them to try to create their own jokes. There are two objects of interest: socks and sweets (though the children may not be immediately aware of this). The final joke combines the two.

The techniques involve:
– playing with words (as in *soccer*);
– using homophones (as in *shoo/shoe*) to create double meanings;
– using homonyms (as in *Sock it to him!*) also to create double meanings;
– playing with sound (as in *sick-sock*).

It would be useful if the children worked in suitable pairs or in small groups (of approximately three members) to read the poems to each other and to help identify the humour.

The children could also work together to create their own jokes. A pair or group, rather than an individual, can sometimes spark more interesting ideas. Suggestions for homophones are given on the activity sheet, though the children could also think of their own. While the children are not expected to create sophisticated jokes, they should try to make coherent sentences or questions (if possible using the common stylistic conventions of jokes) as well as recognise the relationship between the two words. For example, a child might say:
What did the potato say to the bean? Where have you been?

Further activities

Ask the children to identify the links between the two sets of jokes (socks and sweets) and the significance of the final joke.

Ask the children in their groups or with partners to decide what 'a play on words' and 'double meaning' are.

Provide some entertaining children's joke books, such as the *Ha Ha Bonk Book*, for the children to use as inspiration.

Resources

AS 'Just a joke'; *Ha Ha Bonk Book* by Janet and Allan Ahlberg (Puffin)

Just a joke

Name: .... **Date:** ....

Can you make your own jokes? Try making some with these words.

bean/been   dear/deer   sale/sail

Sounds and nonsense

Learning objectives

Text level

- *To use humorous verse as a structure for children to write their own by adaptation, mimicry or substitution; to invent own … nonsense sentences, etc., derived from reading; write tongue-twisters or alliterative sentences; select words with care, rereading and listening to their effect.*

Activity sheet/Expectations

This clever and humorous poem by Edwin Morgan has become a classic, loved by adults and children alike. Quite small children respond to the sounds and playful rhythm and will create their own sounds and words spontaneously. The poem can therefore be used as a model as well as enjoyed.

The children should begin by reading the poem aloud to themselves or, preferably, to a partner. For some it may be a tongue twister, but the insistent and rolling beat should help the children progress through the poem. It does not matter if they make mistakes when reading the words.

They could try to work out what the last word (*CHRYSANTHEMUM*) is and note its link with the expression *Merry Christmas*.

The children should also try to understand that the choice of words and patterning in the poem relates to the computer's inability to process the message *Merry Christmas*, as well as its ability to play with words.

The children are asked to write their own poem, 'Happy Birthday', along similar lines. This is challenging but some help is given. The word *day* gives the children a rhyming structure for their poems, and allows them to focus on creating nonsense words and using the rhythm of 'The computer's first Christmas card'.

Other words that rhyme with *birth* and that the children could use or adapt, might be: *bird, kerb, curl, girl, thirst, first, purse, nurse, purr, stir, burn, fern, worm, work, worse, worst, word.*

Further activities

Ask the children to make up their own tongue twisters using the same *ir* sound (as in *birth*). For example: *thirty twirling girls, thirty twirling curls.*

Resources

AS 'The computer's first Christmas card'; other sound poems by Edwin Morgan, such as 'French Persian cats having a ball' in *Collected Poems 1949–1989* (Carcanet Press Ltd)

The computer's first Christmas card

jollymerry
hollyberry
jollyberry
merryholly
happyjolly
jollyjelly
jellybelly
bellymerry
hollyheppy
jollyMolly
merryJerry
merryHarry
hoppyBarry
heppyJarry
boppyheppy
berryjorry
jorryjolly
moppyjelly
Mollymerry
Jerryjolly
bellyboppy
jorryhoppy

hollymoppy
Barrymerry
Jarryheppy
happyboppy
boppyjolly
jollymerry
merrymerry
merrymerry
merryChris
ammerryas a
Chrismerry
asMERRY CHR
YSANTHEMUM

by Edwin Morgan

1. Can you make a poem with the message 'Happy Birthday'?

2. Jot down some rhyming words and nonsense words.
Here are some to start you off.
Happy birthday
Hippy Thursday
Natty skirtday
Knitty workday

Notes and non-fiction texts

Learning objectives

Text level
- *To make simple notes from non-fiction texts, e.g. keywords and phrases.*
- *To write non-fiction texts, using texts read as models for own writing, e.g. use of headings, sub-headings, captions.*
- To understand what a paragraph is and use simple paragraphs in writing.

Activity sheet/Expectations

The activity sheet focuses on a non-fiction text of three paragraphs about snakes. The first paragraph gives information about snakes in general, the second is about the grass snake and the third about the python. The readability level is approximately nine years. The children therefore need to be confident readers and writers.

There are several other skills involved that require some degree of sophistication. The children need to:
- isolate key points in the text;
- recognise paragraphs;
- understand that each paragraph focuses on something different but related to the topic;
- write brief paragraphs (of two or three sentences) from the work they have done;
- understand how to include headings and sub-headings.

In paragraph one there is less important information (such as the comparison between snakes and other reptiles) and the children should try to underline keywords and phrases. In the remaining paragraphs most points are relevant. For example:
- in paragraph one: *reptiles, cold-blooded, keep their body heat the same;*
- in paragraph two: *grass snake is shy, lives in woods, near streams, lays eggs;*
- in paragraph three: *lives in Africa, strangles its prey, coils round her eggs.*

Further activities

Ask the children to draw an illustration of a snake (for example, the female python guarding her eggs) and write a caption for it. This can be included with their writing.

The children can research additional information about snakes and present the key points differently. For example, as a series of pictures with captions. The children could present their work for others to read.

Note: Simple non-fiction texts, which use headings, sub-headings, glossaries and indexes are useful. The texts need to be well within the children's capabilities so that they can gain an overview of a text as well as scan for specific information.

Resources

AS 'Snakes'; coloured pens; non-fiction texts for research; computer and CD-ROMs for research

Snakes

Snakes are reptiles. They are like lizards and crocodiles. They are like turtles and tortoises. We call them 'cold blooded'. This does not mean their blood is cold! It means that to keep their body heat the same they move between warm places and cool places. When it is very hot they find a cool place. This might be under a rock. When it is cold they lie in the morning sun.

The grass snake is shy. It lives in woods and near streams and lays about 20 eggs at a time. Yes, snakes lay eggs! The grass snake lays its eggs in damp leaves where the baby grass snakes will hatch.

The python is much bigger than the grass snake. It lives in Africa and also likes to be near water. It is very strong and strangles its prey with powerful muscles. It lays about 50 eggs at a time. The female is a good mother. She coils round her eggs until they hatch.

1. Underline three things about snakes in paragraph one.
Use a red pen.

2. Underline two things about grass snakes in paragraph two.
Use a black pen.

3. Underline two things about the python in paragraph three.
Use a blue pen.

4. Write some paragraphs of your own about snakes. Use the information you have underlined.
First write the heading '**Snakes**' in the correct place. Then write two sub-headings, '**Grass snakes**' and '**The python**' at the beginning of your paragraphs.

Objectives grid

	Word	Page	Sentence	Page	Text	Page
T1	Vowel phonemes and digraphs	4	Revising and using capitalisation	8	Writing simple instructions	10, 20
	Homophones	6	Recognising exclamation marks	8	Understanding time and sequential relationships	12
			Using capital letters and full stops	8	Writing about own experiences	14
			Using simple organisational devices	10	Using language of time	16
			Finding linking words and phrases	12, 14	Using simple poetry structures	18
			Understanding that most stories have a message or moral	12	Using structures to write a poem	18
			Rereading own writing	22	Maintaining rhythm and rhyme	18
					Noting key structural features	20
					Using appropriate register in writing instructions	22
					Reading simple instructions	22
T2	Digraph 'wh', 'ph', 'ch'	24	Understanding the need for grammatical agreement	28	Identifying patterns of rhythm and rhyme	32
	Distinguish sounds	24	Using verb tenses	28	Using poem structures as a basis for writing	32, 40
	Create questions	24	Using commas in a list	30	Recognising when the reading aloud makes sense and is effective	34
	Split compound words	26	Reading aloud	30	Writing a brief commentary	34
	Nonsense definitions	26	Using commas	30	Identifying features of sound	34
			Writing using exclamation marks	30	Using story settings from reading	36
					Classifying stories	36
					Using a table to classify information	36
					Identifying story genre	36
					Writing character profiles	38
					Identifying keywords	38
					Using dictionaries and glossaries	42
					Using alphabetical texts	42
					Writing alphabetically	42
T3	Syllables	44	Comparing forms of questions	48	Reading about authors	50, 52
	Polysyllabic words	44	Writing questions and answers	48	Writing a blurb	52
	Common suffixes	46			Reading and collecting humorous poetry	54
	Common prefixes	46			Using humorous verse to write own adaptation	54, 56
					Discussing words and phrases that create humour	56, 58
					Inventing jokes	58
					Understanding what 'play on words' means	60
					Understanding what 'double meaning' means	60
					Making simple notes	62
					Writing non-fiction texts	62
					Understanding what a paragraph is	62